Puffin Books

Making Presents and Other Things

Stuck for a birthday present for someone special? Short of
pocket money at Christmas time? Feeling like brightening
up your room or decorating your table for a party – then
this is the book for you. As well as producing very
acceptable and unusual presents to give your family and
friends, or even keep yourself – you have all the fun of
making them. Turn an old pair of jeans into a handbag:
make a Money Mouse, a Ring Thing and Curl Clips
(which are not at all what they might seem to be). There
are Sparkling Roses to inspire you; delicious
Marshmallow Snowmen, and edible pictures; Roller
People and Jitter Bugs, pendants, pictures and party
pieces to delight you.

The instructions are easy to follow and illustrated with
diagrams in colour and black and white to help you. With
a little patience and lots of imagination you will discover
how easy it is to make these lovely presents and
decorations, and surprise your delighted friends and
relatives with your talent.

Making Presents and Other Things

by Belinda Price

illustrated by Robin Lawrie

Puffin Books

Puffin Books
Penguin Books Ltd,
Harmondsworth, Middlesex, England
Penguin Books,
625 Madison Avenue, New York, New York 10022, U.S.A.
Penguin Books Australia Ltd,
Ringwood, Victoria, Australia
Penguin Books Canada Ltd,
41 Steelcase Road West, Markham, Ontario, Canada
Penguin Books (N.Z.) Ltd,
182–190 Wairau Road, Auckland 10, New Zealand

First published 1976
Text copyright © Belinda Price, 1976
Illustrations copyright © Robin Lawrie, 1976

Filmset in 'Monophoto' Baskerville 11 on 12 pt by
Richard Clay (The Chaucer Press), Ltd, Bungay, Suffolk
and printed in Great Britain by
Fletcher & Son Ltd, Norwich

Contents

A Word from the Author

There's nothing nicer than actually *making* presents for people. Not only do they appreciate them, but you have all the fun of making them.

Some of the presents in this book are quite difficult to make, so I have awarded them all stars – one star for the easy ones to three stars for the hardest ones. I've tried to include something for everyone – mother, father, brothers and sisters – young and old, aunts, uncles and friends. Some presents are useful, some are purely decorative, some are just fun to make and you'll probably want to keep them. I hope you will.

A Blossom Tree*

You need: small cream carton, filled with earth or sand
a well-shaped small branch off a tree
silver or gold paint or spray
tissue paper
rubber solution glue
decorative paper

This is a really simple-to-make tree, covered in bright blossom.

Take some time and trouble to look for a well-shaped branch about 36 cm (14 ins) high. It must have lots of little twigs and shoots to which you can fix your blossom.

Fill your cream carton with damp earth or sand and push your branch in firmly. Then paint the entire branch or spray it with silver or gold aerosol. If you can spray it out of doors, on newspaper, there is much less likelihood of your making a mess. If you are spraying indoors, make quite sure that everywhere near you is well covered with paper. Leave the paint to dry, then cover the carton with a decorative paper or with aluminium foil.

7

Next, cut out several circles of tissue paper, about 6 cm ($2\frac{1}{2}$ ins) diameter. To save time, fold your tissue paper over many times so that you can cut out lots of circles at once.

Make a hole through the centre of each circle. Put a little dab of glue around the hole of one of the circles, and, starting at the bottom of the tree, thread the circle gently on to a twig, with the glued side facing you. Push it down the twig about a centimetre or so, then pinch the centre together at the back of the flower to form a tight stem. Still holding the stem in one hand, carefully fluff out the flower a little with the other hand.

Cover the whole tree in this way, until it is a mass of blossom. I think one colour of tissue paper used throughout is the most effective.

Camouflaged Clip★★

You need: 1 wooden clothes-peg
1 cork table mat (or very strong board that will not bend)
enamel paint
strong glue

This is an easy way to make a useful present (a clip for keeping together bills or unanswered letters or licences, etc.) that looks something special.

First cut the cork table mat (or strong cardboard) into two pieces, each measuring 4 cm by 8 cm ($1\frac{1}{2}$ ins by 3 ins). Now paint your clothes-peg. To avoid getting messy, clip the peg to the side of a jar, paint it, and leave it to dry. Also, paint the four edges and one side of both bits of cork. I use enamel paint, which can be bought in tiny pots in a good choice of bright colours from toy/craft/hobby shops.

When the paint is completely dry, cover the top (or bottom) side of the clothes-peg with a generous coating of glue.

Firmly place the peg, glue side down, on to the centre of the painted side of the cork. Cover the top of the peg with more glue and place the second piece of cork, painted side *down*, on to the peg. To help the glue to set really firmly and strongly use a bulldog clip large enough to fit over both pieces of cork. Leave overnight.

Now to decorate the two plain outside pieces of cork. You could glue on some decorative wrapping paper; or paint one side and stick on letters (cut from magazines) to form the words SHOPPING LIST or GRANDMA or REMINDERS etc.

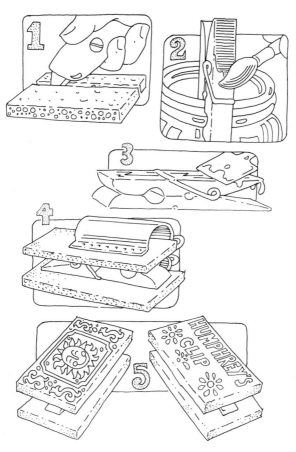

Owl***

You need: 1 empty plastic lemon
1 ping-pong ball
1 lavatory-paper tube
a twig
felt
glue
plaster of Paris
enamel paint
poster paint

This owl is not useful in any way. There is nothing hidden under his feathers, he is just a lovely ornament.

For the stump of the tree, cut 4 cm (1½ ins) off a lavatory-paper tube and paint the outside a dark colour. Make a hole on either side of the tube, about half way down but at a slight angle, and push a twig through this to make the stump more realistic.

To make the owl's head, unscrew the lid of a plastic lemon, make a small hole in a ping-pong ball and gently ease it on to the 'bump' of the lemon, where the lid fitted, until the ball fits tightly over it.

With a sharp pair of scissors, cut out wing shapes on either side of the lemon, and divide each wing into four feathers, each about 4 cm (1½ ins) in length.

Mix up about 85 gms (3 ozs) plaster of Paris with 1½

10

tablespoons of water and pour this into the up-turned stump until it is completely full. Then gently press the end of the lemon into it, making sure that some of the plaster mixture goes right into the base of the lemon, as this will ensure that the owl will set into the plaster and will then stand up firmly. (You can look through the wings to check.)

With a sharp-pointed knife, or a warm one, make two slits in the ping-pong ball at the top of the head, about 10 mm ($\frac{1}{2}$ in.) each in length, for the ears, and another in the face for the beak. Then paint the whole head and the inside of the wings with enamel paint.

If possible, choose three colours of felt to cover the owl to make him really eye-catching. Try brown, orange and yellow together (with an orange painted head), or purple, lilac and pink (with a lilac coloured head).

First of all, cover the eight 'feathers' on the wings with the darkest of the three felts you have chosen. If you have some pinking shears, cut the 'feathers' with these, and then glue them on. Next, starting again with the darkest colour, cut two strips of felt to match the width of the lemon body and measuring about 15 mm ($\frac{3}{4}$ in.) the other way. Cut v-shapes out all along the length of the felt at the bottom edge, then dab a line of glue all along the top edge. Press this on to the lemon body, so that the frilled edge comes to just below the top of the tree trunk (to hide the join). Do the same with the second strip you cut on the other side of the owl.

Next, cut two strips of your second colour (one for the

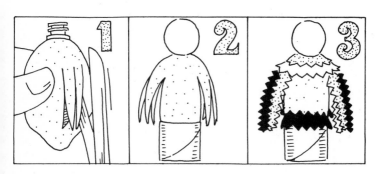

front, one for the back), again measuring the width, and cutting it 15 mm ($\frac{3}{4}$ in.) in length. Cut out the v-shapes along the bottom, glue along the top edge and press it on so that the frills come over the top of the feathers on the wings.

Now you have another three layers to complete the body, one of each colour. You may have to cut slits in the felt on the opposite side to the frills, so that when you glue the felt down, the slits will overlap rather than gather.

Cut out two large circles for the eyes, two ear shapes and a beak from the darkest colour felt (to match the wings), and glue these on with glue. Use a cocktail stick to help you to push the ears and beak in properly. To make the eyes really show up, cut out two smaller circles of your second colour, and two even smaller of your third colour and glue them one on top of the other on to the first circle.

Exotics ★ ★

You need: an empty plastic lemon
glue and paint
split peas, or pasta shapes, or dried flowers, or sequins

An empty plastic squeezy lemon can be decorated to look just like a very exotic egg, but it is much easier to handle.

First you have to get rid of the 'bump' made by the lid (see illustration). Unscrew the cap and pull out the inner covering (the piece with the little hole through which the lemon is squeezed). Keep this carefully. Cut off the whole piece just below the cap, and push the inner covering back into the hole; this should fit exactly.

I think the easiest decoration to start with is split peas. Simply cover the lemon, a little patch at a time, with glue,

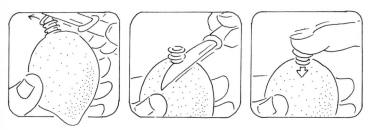

and stick on the split peas, as close together as possible, until none of the lemon base is visible. When the glue has dried and the peas are really set, you can paint the whole thing, with enamel, or nail varnish, or gold or silver aerosol. If you are using aerosol paint be sure to cover the surrounding areas with newspaper.

Try some of the other pasta shapes: small macaroni glued all over the lemon, and then painted gold, looks very exotic; little pasta circles painted only on the outer edges; or paint the lemon first and stick small dried flowers all over it.

At some dressmaking counters you can buy packets of sequins. These look lovely arranged as a pattern glued on to a dark painted lemon. The variety of possible decorations is enormous and you can really let yourself go.

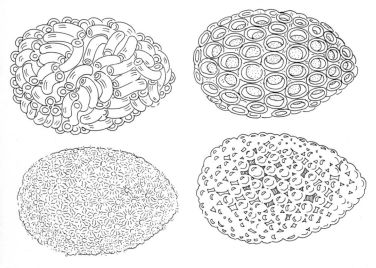

A Tidy Tray*

You need: polystyrene tray
             old newspaper or comic
             wallpaper paste
             little pictures or stamps for collage
             or paint and braid

Look out for some of these polystyrene trays in supermarkets, or chain stores. They are used in the packaging of chicken pieces, meat loaves, fish, fruit, vegetables etc. The idea is to cover them in papier mâché. When dry and decorated they make extremely useful little containers to hold those paper clips, erasers, pencils, pens and other bits and pieces that lie around untidily on a desk; or your hair slides, safety pins and so on, on the dressing table.

Choose carefully the right size and shaped tray. One containing a meat loaf, with a base measuring 8 cm × 17 cm (3 ins × 6¾ ins) makes an excellent desk tidy as it is long enough and deep enough to hold scissors as well as plenty of pens and pencils. A little tray 13 cm × 4 cm × 2 cm (5 ins × 1½ ins × ¾ in.) will take hair slides, rubber bands and clips.

Prepare the papier mâché by tearing newspaper into bits roughly 4 cm × 2 cm (1½ ins × ¾ in.). As you need four or five layers on your tray, make a separate pile from torn up comics. Put on a layer of comic paper, then a layer of newspaper, and you will find it is much easier to keep count of how many layers you have put on. Make up a jam jar of paste by filling the jar almost to the top with cold water and sprinkling on to it one teaspoonful of wallpaper paste. Put the lid on the jar and shake hard until the powder is dissolved.

Cover the inside of the tray with the paste and stick down one layer of paper, carefully overlapping each piece of paper. The paper must go right over the edge of the tray (you can cut it straight later). Continue in this way until you

14

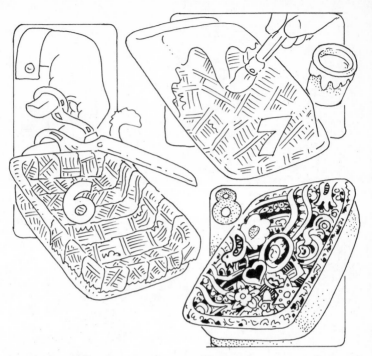

have put on five layers of paper. Remember to use plenty of glue as this will add strength to the container.

Now leave the tray to dry. (Be patient – it may take a week.) Do not put it in a very warm place or the paper is apt to rise and make the base of the tray bumpy. When the papier mâché is completely dry, you should be able to lift it gently out of the polystyrene tray. If this does not work, then break off bits of the polystyrene until you can get it out. The centre may still be damp, so do let it dry thoroughly. With a sharp pair of scissors, cut around the outside edge to straighten it and to give it a good finish.

Now decorate the tray. You could make a collage for the inside by cutting out lots of tiny pictures from magazines and glueing them on – or you could cover the inside with cut-out letters or used stamps. Then paint the outside. Alternatively, paint the entire tray, and add your own designs in a contrasting colour, and stick some braid around the edge.

Jeans Bag**

You need: an old pair of jeans or corduroys
strong thread (button thread if possible)
large press fasteners or *Velcro*

An old pair of jeans or corduroy trousers can be worn out at
the knees but not at the seat of the pants, and this part can
be made into a good size bag with useful pockets. You can
make a very simple bag or a more elaborate one.

1. Cut the legs off the jeans about 6 cm (2½ ins) below the
crutch.

2. Unpick the stitches between the inside of the legs.

3. Measure the length between the top and the bottom
centre front A to B.

4. Mark the same measurements at both sides of the jeans (C
and D) and mark and cut a straight line from B to C and from
B to D.

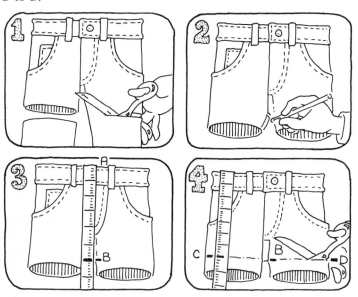

5. Turn the jeans inside out and tack the back and front together along the base. Then sew them together with backstitch, preferably with button thread. To finish off neatly, oversew the raw edge.

6. Turn right side out again, and carefully unpick the zip, cutting it off at the waistband. Pin the fly down and sew it either with back stitching or with little hem stitches. The button at the waist can be replaced with a really special one.

7. If you want to use the outer pockets for money, train passes etc., I should sew large poppers (or a little *Velcro*) to the top of each pocket. Do the same for the bag opening.

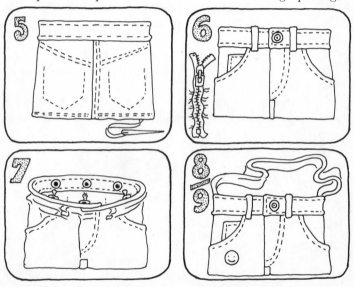

8. For the shoulder strap, either buy a length of decorative braid or strong ribbon (about 61 cm [2 ft]); or make a strap from the legs that have been cut off.

9. Cut two strips (36 cm × 10 cm [14 ins × 4 ins]) from the back of the trouser legs. Backstitch the pieces together making one long strip. Fold this strip in half longways and sew together all down the long side and across the bottom edge. Now turn this strip inside out and sew it in place.

To decorate the bag sew on a favourite badge.

18

Ornamental Garden Lights[*]

You need: (*per light*)

    2 round aluminium foil dishes (about 16 cm [6¼ ins] across)

    1 night light, or small fat candle

    1 wire coat hanger

    some fuse wire, or very fine wire

Here is an easy way of making decorative lights to hang in the garden for Hallowe'en, or for a bonfire party, or late evening birthday party.

First, cut an openwork pattern in the flat bottom of one of the foil dishes with a pair of pointed scissors. The light will shine through the holes you cut (start with something simple like small triangles). Now rest the night light or candle on the inside base of the second foil dish. Make a tiny hole in the aluminium on either side of the light, about half way up. Thread a 20-cm (8-ins) piece of fuse wire through these two holes from the outside and twist the ends together around the 'waist' of the light to secure it.

Lay the patterned foil dish on top of the one with the light

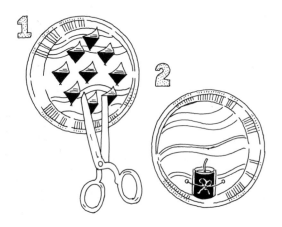

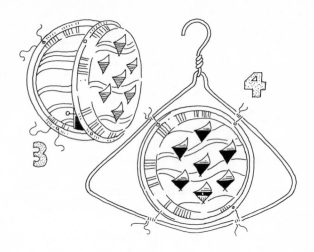

in it, and make holes through the outer rim of both dishes in four places (top, bottom and two sides). Thread about 20 cm (8 ins) of wire through each set of holes and twist firmly together. Don't cut off the left-over ends of wire. Lay the dish in the centre of the frame of a wire coat hanger (night light at the bottom centre) and attach it by twisting the four left-over bits of wire around the coat hanger frame.

The wire coat hanger is not strictly necessary and you could hang up the lights by making a simple handle from fuse wire and threading this through the top; but I use the frame to secure the lights if there is any wind. A little fuse wire twisted around the frame in three or four places will fix the light on to whatever tree or post you hang them.

When you have made one light in this way, you can experiment with other shapes and sizes of foil dishes, and also make different patterns for the light to shine through – perhaps lots of small holes, or several stars. Make a hole near the wick of the night light, so that you can light it easily.

Always use *wire* for securing both the night light and the dishes, and a *wire* coat hanger, as these are flame proof. Incidentally, the foil dishes protect the flame from being blown out by the wind.

Useful Boxes[*]

You need: empty shoe box
       1 m 22 cms (4 ft) braid or ribbon
       empty matchboxes

Here is an exciting way of giving someone lots of sensible and practical bits and pieces and at the same time it is great fun to make.

First, find an empty shoe box (the smaller the better as it is easier to fill) and about 1 m 22 cms (4 ft) of braid or ribbon for the handle. Cut four slits wide enough to slot the ribbon through, on both the long sides of the box in the centre, two slits, A + D, 5 mm (¼ in.) from the base, and the other two slits, B + C, 5 mm (¼ in.) below the box lid. Now, thread the ribbon through, from the outside of the box at B, from the inside to the outside at A, bring it under the outside of the box and thread it through to the inside at D, and to the outside again at C. Join the ribbon ends at the top with a small knot, or sew them together. This will make a strong handle.

Now line the inside of the box by glueing odd bits of wallpaper or wrapping paper to the base and four sides. Decorate the outside of the box with little pictures cut from magazines or wrapping paper. On the lid of the box write SO AND SO'S USEFUL BOX.

You should fill the box with all those useful bits and pieces that can never be found when you really need them. Here are some ideas: pencil; note pad; luggage tags; eraser; sticky tape; stamp hinges; photograph corners; paper fasteners; drawing pins; rubber bands; small ruler; pins; paper clips; gummed economy labels; glue; safety pins; cardboard badges; string; scissors; chalk; gumstrip sealing tape; magic letters (rub down); self-adhesive labels (which come in all sorts of colours and shapes); gummed border labels; gummed paper stars; cloth (or gummed) reinforcement rings; letter or

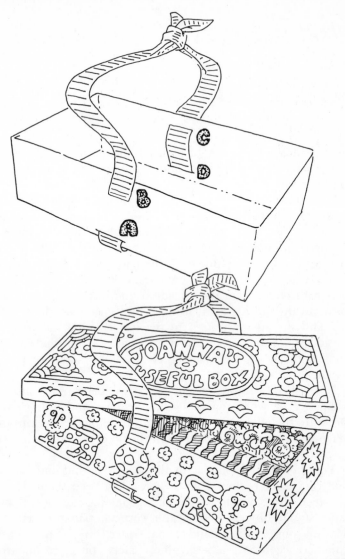

bulldog clips; sealing wax; map tacks; glass-headed pins. (All these can be found in newsagents and stationers.)

To keep all these little things tidy in the Useful Box, find some empty matchboxes, cover each one with some pretty

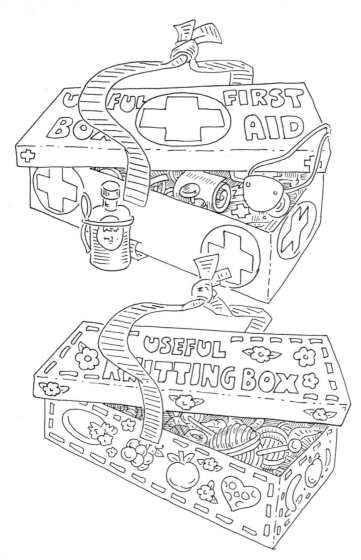

sticky-backed plastic and clearly label it. There are lots of other ideas for these boxes, and I am sure that you can think up some of your own. For instance, to someone longing to knit you could give a 'Useful Knitting Box'. Put in one or two pairs of knitting needles; odd balls of wool; some blunt-ended wool needles (with a large eye); a tape measure; a stitch holder and a knitting register (to keep count of the rows). There is a Ladybird book *About Knitting* which you could also put in as it explains how to make the stitches and includes simple patterns. They also have a *Learning to Sew* book, so you could make up a 'Useful Sewing Box'. (There is a list inside the book of the materials, etc., that you would need to buy in order to practise sewing and to make up some of the ideas.)

For someone interested in science, why not give one of the Ladybird *Junior Science Books*. There is a list of articles needed for the experiments in the book given in the front. So collect these together for a 'Useful Science Box'.

Make a 'Useful First-Aid Box' for a friend who likes to play hospitals. Fill decorated matchboxes with cotton wool, plasters and pieces of lint or gauze (all clearly labelled and marked with a red cross). Fill a small polythene bottle with coloured water (to do this, add a little food colouring to the water) and label THE MEDICINE *2 spoonfuls 3 times a day*. Attach a plastic teaspoon with an elastic band. Make an eye patch with a small piece of black felt and elastic; cut a finger off a rubber glove for a finger stall; make up a few bandages from an old sheet or pillowcase. Your doctor may let you have an old syringe for injections (without the needle of course). You could also include one or two cardboard badges marked DOCTOR and NURSE, and a plain pad. Mark the pad PRESCRIPTIONS and include some tiny envelopes.

For someone ill in bed (or in hospital) give a 'Useful Make and Do Box'. Put in lots of sheets of plain paper; some card: coloured sticky paper and coloured sticky paper shapes; tissue paper; glue; pipe cleaners; scissors, envelopes; and one or two things for imaginary play like restaurant pads, petty cash vouchers and cloakroom tickets (all again from stationers).

Think also of ideas for a 'Car Journey Box'; a 'Cooking Box'; a 'Chemical Garden Box'; a 'Printing Box'.

Marshmallow Snowman*

You need: 5 white marshmallows per person
icing sugar
2 cocktail sticks
cake decorations or small sweets
small paper plate or foil dish, or jelly case
paper and glue

Marshmallow snowmen are place markers for a special occasion like Christmas or a winter birthday party and also make a good present for your friends. Make one for each guest, who can then either eat it or take it home. It is best to make them early in the day of the party, so that the 'glue' has time to set and all the decorations will stay firmly in place.

Mix up a thick paste of three tablespoons of icing sugar and a very little water. Cut the sharp point off one end of a cocktail stick and on to the other end thread four marshmallows through their centres. Put some icing sugar 'glue' on the base of the marshmallow which has the blunt end of the stick in it (but not poking out) and press the whole thing down firmly on to the paper plate, or small foil dish (or even a piece of strong card, or jelly or cake case). Cut the fifth

marshmallow in half and glue the halves to either side of the second marshmallow from the top to make the snowman's arms.

To decorate the snowman, use tiny sweets for his face and buttons, or little balls used for cake decorations, and stick them all on with icing-sugar glue. The top hat can be made from a large chocolate drop with a liquorice 'chimney' shape up-ended on top; and if you can get it, cut off a bit of liquorice shoe lace for his scarf and his stick (tiny little pieces are good for his nose and his mouth).

Write your guest's name on a small piece of paper. With real glue, fix it to one end of a cocktail stick, and push the other end into his arm.

A Very Special
Useful Box*

You need: 1 shoe box
        rice paper
        wafer biscuits
        cake colouring
        icing sugar
        paint brush
        edible bits and pieces

Here is an idea for an original present for a friend when you cannot think what else to give him or her. You fill up a useful box with all sorts of things that can be made into a picture and then the entire picture, paper glue and all can be eaten!

First of all decorate the useful box, as on page 21, but leave the inside of the lid blank because you will need to stick the instructions on it.

Into the box put rice paper (from most newsagents and some grocers), some icing sugar well wrapped in a bag or carton and labelled; two or three packets of wafer biscuits (from most ice cream shops); some food colouring used for cake decorations; a very thin paint brush; a variety of little sweets, preferably soft ones that can be cut up – jelly babies or jelly teddies; currants, nuts, glacé cherries and cake decorations can all add to the fun. You can put all of these into separate matchboxes, decorated and labelled. If your box is small and the rice paper will not fit in, do not cut or fold it but give it separately.

Now for the instructions. The 'paper' to work on is the rice paper; 'glue' is a little icing sugar mixed to a thickish paste with water, added drop by drop. The wafer biscuits can be cut with scissors or a blunt knife into virtually any

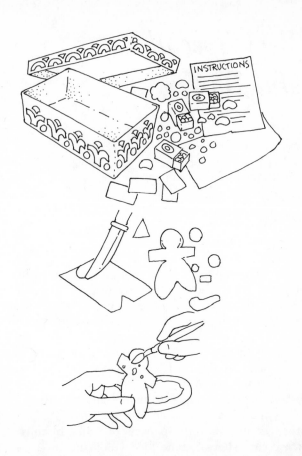

shape: houses, animals, figures, trees, stars, letters and numbers. When the shape is cut from the wafer spread a little 'glue' on gently with a knife and press it on to the rice paper. The picture can be 'painted' with edible food colouring, put on with the thin paint brush, but not too liberally or both rice paper and the wafer will dissolve. The sweets and other bits and pieces can be used for all sorts of things and add a good deal of colour and variety to the picture, as well as fun.

Why not make up a 'Very Special Useful Box' for your brother or sister or cousin and hint that you would like one for your Christmas or birthday present?

29

Money Mouse ★★★

You need: an empty plastic lemon

a piece of stretchy material, 24 cm × 30 cm (9½ ins × 11¾ ins)

a piece of felt, 5 cm × 3 cm (2 ins × 1¼ in.)

2 coloured glass-headed pins

about 16 cm (6¼ ins) of black button or strong thread

a strong clear adhesive glue

Make this little mouse to look after your pennies. Believe it or not, he started out in life as a plastic lemon.

First, prepare the lemon by getting rid of the 'bump' made by the lid (see diagram on p. 13). Unscrew the lid, and pull out the inner tightly fitting cap, the piece with the little hole through which the lemon is squeezed (use a sharp-pointed knife to ease it out). Keep this cap carefully. Now cut off the projection immediately below the last ridge. The inner cap can now be pushed back into the hole.

When you look at the lemon, you will notice a line running right through the centre of it. Using this as a guide for the central dividing line, cover one half only of the lemon with a very thin layer of glue, taking care not to go over the dividing line. Put the lemon in your left hand, between thumb and first finger, glued side uppermost, and place your material on top, with about 6 cm (2½ ins) hanging over on three sides, and the rest on the fourth side. Then gently pull the material down tightly over the lemon until you are holding it in one hand in a tight bunch covering the lemon. Keep holding it tightly like this until the glue sets on the material. You will see now why you need a fairly stretchy material to cover the mouse. Seersucker, or a very fine, lightweight cotton or crepe are the best materials to use, because, by pulling it tightly, you will not get too many creases around the central dividing line.

When the glue is set, turn the lemon upside down and cut the material away just below the central dividing line.

Cover the second half of the lemon in glue and put the material on in exactly the same way as you did the first half. When you have cut the surplus material away, right up to the dividing line, make sure all the end bits of the material are glued down firmly, so that they do not fray. A cocktail stick is very useful here for putting on tiny bits of glue.

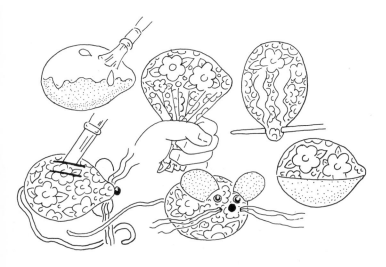

Now the fun starts: give your mouse some character! The top side of the mouse is the part with writing on the lemon (you can feel this through the material). Holding the mouse right side up, push in the two coloured glass-headed pins, about 1 cm ($\frac{1}{2}$ in.) apart, and 1 cm ($\frac{1}{2}$ in.) above the central dividing line. Cut out two ear shapes from the piece of felt (try to choose a good contrasting colour to the mouse's body), and put a little dab of glue at the base of each ear, before pressing them on just above the eyes, at a slight angle. Also from the felt cut out a very small circle for the nose, and glue it on. Or use black felt if you have it.

Now, very carefully, with a heated darning needle, make two holes in the dividing line about 1 cm ($\frac{1}{2}$ in.) on either side of the nose, for the whiskers, and another for the tail in the back of the mouse roughly where the hole is in the inner cap. (You can make these holes through the material of the mouse's body.) Just a word of warning though – if you are using a hot skewer or knitting needle, wear gloves or be sure the end you are holding is well insulated.

For the whiskers, cut five or six pieces of black button thread, each 10 cm (4 ins) long, and thread them through the two holes on either side of the nose, with a small darning needle. With a cocktail stick, put a dab of glue at the entrance to these two holes to seal the whiskers into place.

Use the 16 cm (6¼ ins) of string (or wool) for a tail, and with a cocktail stick push it into the hole you have already made at the back. Seal the entrance with a dab of glue.

To enable your mouse to guard your pennies, turn him upside down, and with a very sharp pair of pointed scissors, cut two lines 5 mm (¼ in.) on either side of an imaginary central line running from nose to tail), both about 4 cm (1½ ins) long. Through one of these slits, push in your pennies. The weight of even one or two pennies will help the mouse to balance well. And don't worry, you can get the money out again the same way without having to destroy the mouse.

Flower Pot Tree*

You need: 1 plastic flower pot
            1 strong stick
            1 cream or yoghurt carton
            tissue paper
            rubber solution glue
            a little foil

A little tree covered in blossom makes a lovely present to cheer up someone who is ill, and it can add bright colour to anyone's room.

First, wrap the cream or yoghurt carton in foil and fill it with earth or sand or plaster of Paris. Push in the stick very firmly (I used a 15 cm [6 ins] stick with an 8 cm [3 ins] flower pot).

Balance the pot on the stick and then cover it completely with tissue flowers. To do this, cut your tissue paper in 8 cm. (3 ins) squares. Find the centre of the square, put a dab of glue in the middle of the tissue, and pinch it together to make a minute 'stem'. Then hold the stem whilst you fluff out the rest of the tissue. Put another dab of glue on the top centre of the flower pot and press the stem of the flower on firmly. Continue in this way until the whole pot is completely covered in blossom.

You can colour your tree in one colour of tissue or mix your colours – or you could make an entirely silver tree using silver foil paper.

Roller People and
Roller Animals***

You need: (*for each roller person*)
foam cushion rollers – 1 medium and 4 small
1 ping-pong ball
1 pipe cleaner
2 corks
glue
bits of material

NB. If you are making animals you will need extra rollers.

Foam cushion rollers for curling hair (sold in most chain and department stores) can be fitted together to make all sorts of people and animals with movable arms and legs. These can be dressed or painted and used to make a circus, a zoo, a crib scene, *Magic Roundabout* figures, a mascot doll, etc.

Buy two sizes of foam rollers to start with, medium and small. You will use one medium roller and four small for each person you make, but for the animals you will need an extra roller or two.

To make the roller doll remove the plastic frames from the four small rollers, but leave in the plastic centre rods. You will notice that one end of each rod is more rounded than the other. This rounded end will clip on to the plastic frame of the body (the medium size roller). Fit the four small rollers on this way, two for arms, two for legs.

For the head use a ping-pong ball. With a hot skewer, make two holes at A and B, thread a pipe cleaner through the two holes and twist two or three times together at the base of the ball to secure.

The plastic rod in the centre of the roller body is also more rounded at one end. Make this the top end of the body and twist the two pipe cleaner ends around the plastic frame to

35

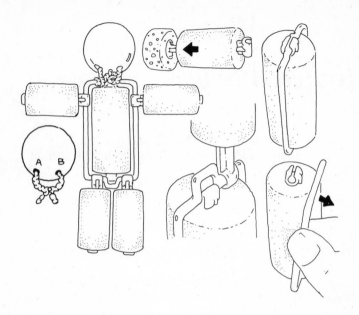

fix the head on, keeping it as close to the central rod as possible.

To help the roller doll to stand, make two feet by cutting off about 10 mm ($\frac{1}{2}$ in.) from the tops of two corks, and about 5 mm ($\frac{1}{4}$ in.) of foam off the base of the legs (remove the foam from the plastic rod to do this).

Make a hole in the centre of each bit of cork big enough to push the central rod in. Glue both foam legs firmly to the cork bases, pushing the rod well in.

The animal bodies are made in the same way, but the heads and necks are made from foam rollers with both the plastic frame and the rod removed. Thread a pipe cleaner through the centre of these rollers, twisting one end around the frame (as with the ping-pong ball head for the person). Secure the other end inside the animal's head with glue.

This gives you the basic idea of how to make the people and animals. If you want to dress the people, unclip the arms and legs and glue material to each roller. To cover the body roller, unclip the bottom of the frame and slip the roller off the central rod. Cover it, slip the roller on again and clip the rod back.

To finish off the arms, glue two felt handshapes together with a bit of the arm rod in between, and gently ease the foam over the end of the felt. Whatever you do remember not to cover the plastic frame around the roller body, otherwise you will not be able to clip the arms and legs on again. If you do want to make a long dress or coat, leave a hole where the arms clip in.

You can cut the rollers to shape the animals' heads and glue the foam together (for a snout perhaps) holding it in place with a bulldog clip until the glue dries. Cotton wool, thick knitting wool and string make good coats for the animals unless you want to paint them. You can vary the animal's movements by clipping the legs to different parts of the plastic frame body.

Jitter Bugs **

You need: 1 packet of plastic garden labels, 10–12 cm (4–4¾ ins) long
paper fasteners, 2 cm (¾ in.) long
enamel paint
small bits of felt
1 ping-pong ball

By fixing the decorated plastic labels together with the paper fasteners, you can make an exciting, moving toy.

First, using a hot skewer or knitting needle, make holes in the labels just big enough to push a paper fastener in. (Make sure the end of the skewer is well insulated.) Make three holes in six of the labels – one hole in either end and one in the centre. Most labels have a hole in one end already, but you may need to make it bigger to fit the fastener. The seventh label needs a hole in the centre and at one end only.

Paint the plastic labels before they are fixed together, leaving one side to dry completely before painting on the other. I use enamel paint, bought in tiny pots from toy/craft/hobby shops.

Now, assemble the body, starting at the base. Lay one label down, place a second one across it at right angles,

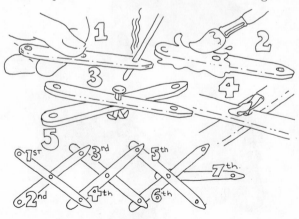

centre hole over centre hole. Push a paper fastener (which *must* be 2 cm [¾ in.] long, not the very small ones) through these two centre holes and open flat at the back. Then bend the prongs of the fastener in half, one over the other, and hammer down firmly. This must be done well, because the points are very sharp.

Next put the bottom end of the third label on to the top end of the second and fix together with a fastener. Put the bottom end of the fourth label on to the top of the first and fix. Join the centre holes of the third and fourth labels together. Now put the fifth and sixth labels on to the third and fourth, and join the centre holes of 5 and 6, *together* with the bottom of the seventh label. Hammer the paper fasteners down very flat and paint them, back and front, the same colours as your labels.

For the face, hands and feet (of the frog or the clown) cut two shapes each from felt, if possible, as this is the easiest material to work in. You can use the shapes the artist has drawn as patterns. If you don't want your creatures to have too long a neck, cut 1–2 cm (½ in.–¾ in.) off the top of the seventh label. Lay the end of the label in between the two pieces of the felt face, right up to the top of the felt head and either sew or glue these together. To fix the felt head on extra firmly, sew with tiny stitches in and out right through the centre hole of the label. This will prevent the head from ever slipping off, and then do the same for the hands and feet.

If you want to make a different sort of 'Jitter Bug', try using a ping-pong ball for a head. Cut a slit not quite as wide as a label, and then jam it on.

A Ring Thing*

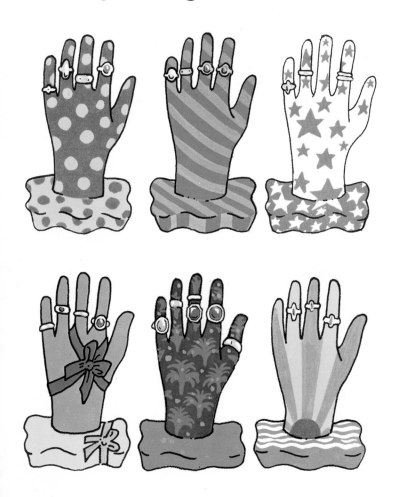

You need: 1 kg (2 lbs) plaster of Paris
          1 small rubber glove
          small cardboard box

An easily made fun hand to hold your rings and bracelets, letters, invitations, etc.

Mix up about three quarters of the plaster of Paris with roughly 2·5 dl (10 oz) of cold water – it should make a thickish cream consistency. If you want a coloured hand, add powder paint or tempera colour to the water before mixing.

Put just under half this mixture into the rubber glove and squeeze it well down into the fingers and thumb. Do this very thoroughly to make sure that there are no air holes. If you hold the glove up to the light, you can see where the plaster has filled in.

Now put the rest of the plaster in and again work it well down to fill in all the air bubbles. Still holding the glove upside down, secure it to the back of a chair, or the edge of a shelf, with a couple of strong bulldog clips.

Leave to dry. This happens very quickly with plaster of Paris, but do not be tempted to look at it too soon. I always leave it well alone for a good hour for safety's sake!

The glove will not come off in one piece (even if you grease the inside first, so this is not worth doing). Cut straight up the centre of the palm to the fingers, but do not hurry to pull the glove off, as the thumb and fingers are very brittle. If by any chance one does break off, you can glue it on again!

Leave the hand to dry overnight, resting on its back.

The next day, prepare the rest of the plaster (coloured if you want) to stand the hand in (300 gm plaster mixed with about 1·5 dl water). Pour this plaster into a small box (I use the top flat half of a cardboard egg container which I have already lined with foil paper) and stand the hand in it, pushing the base of the hand gently but firmly right in. Hold it upright like this until you feel that the plaster is beginning to set and the hand can be left to stand on its own quite safely. Leave it to set where no one will knock it over. After an hour or so, peel away the foil paper together with the egg box and let the plaster get really dry.

You can spray the hand gold or silver (from an aerosol can) or cover it with emulsion or decorate it with your own designs done with felt pens. I paint the base in a contrasting colour. If you want to give the 'Ring Thing' to someone for a present, tie a pretty ribbon around the wrist and buy one or two very cheap rings to adorn the fingers (curtain rings would do), or twist a small piece of tinsel on to one or two fingers. You can paint fingernails on it, or put a piece of real sticking plaster on one of the fingers, or decorate it like the artist has! If you varnish it, leave the varnish to dry for 2–3 hours.

Doily Pinnacles *

You need: stiff card (about 61 sq. cm or 2 ft square)
red foil paper to cover one side
8 paper fasteners or some red raffia or wool
white openwork doilies

This is a simply made Christmas centre piece, but it can be so easily spoilt unless you choose doilies which have a very openwork pattern to give the decoration frothy lightness.

Cut a tall paper cone shape from a quarter circle of stiff card (about 61–76 cm [24–30 ins] radius). On one side only, glue or staple on red foil paper. Punch or skewer equidistant holes along both straight sides, about 1 cm ($\frac{1}{2}$ in.) from the edge (Fig. 3) so that you can overlap and attach together with paper fasteners, or sew through the matching holes with red raffia or wool. With a skewer, make a hole (about the size of a new halfpenny or a little smaller) near the top of the cone. Take a doily and pinch the centre together tightly to form a short 'stem' or about 3 cm ($1\frac{1}{4}$ ins) (Fig. 4). Push this through the hole you have made and, holding it inside the cone with one hand, arrange the lacy part outside. Make the next hole about 6–8 cm ($2\frac{1}{2}$–3 in.) away from the first and continue in this way to cover the entire pinnacle. At the very top, you could put a tinsel star, or a Christmas fairy.

You can now use the pinnacle as it is, or put it over a strong stick, covered in tinsel or foil, which is fixed securely in a container of some sort.

Curl Clips**

You need: a curl clip
            little bits of felt
            glue
            needle and thread

Pretty felt flowers, fruit etc., to clip on to and liven up a T-shirt, a smock, a hat or jeans; or they can be clipped into your hair; or even used as a bookmark. Here are a few designs to start you off.

(The curl clip can be bought in packets from most chain stores, chemists or dressmaking counters.)

46

First, trace the outline of one of these shapes carefully, pin it to a piece of felt and cut it out twice. Sew the two shapes together with tiny oversewing stitches, leaving a gap at the centre top through which you push one of the 'prongs' of the clip up to the 'spring'. Now, press the clip open and with little stitches sew in and out over this gap to fix the felt shape to the clip.

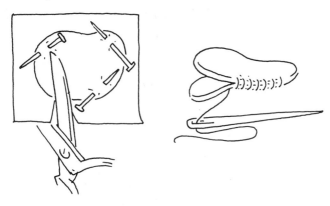

Next, trace and then cut out the decorative part of the shape (preferably in a good contrasting colour) which can be glued to the felt shape, making sure that part of it is covering, and glued to, the top of the curl clip. The top of the clip should not be visible at all.

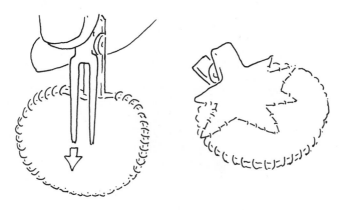

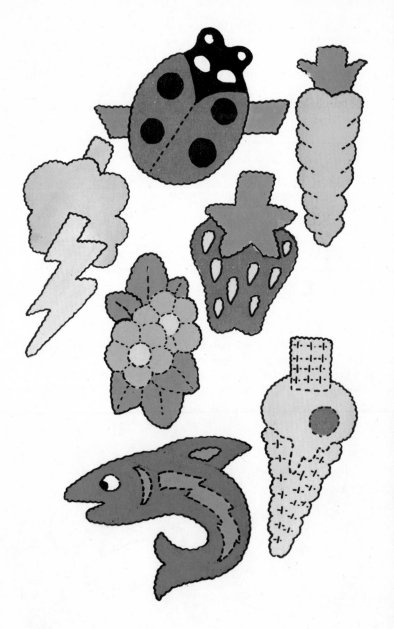

Pendants*

You need: rod or pole rings
little portraits or photographs
thin card
about 70 cm (28 ins) narrow ribbon or tape
all purpose glue

Try making a pendant to hold a picture of your favourite pop or film star, or make a medallion or necklace.

You can buy *Portier Rod Rings* or café curtain rings at any good ironmonger or hardware store, and they are only a few pence each. You can also use *Cornice Pole Rings* (in brass or in wood), but these are much more expensive and much more difficult to get (though you could look out for them on old curtains at sales).

To start, trace around the outside edge of the ring on some thin card, and cut out the shape. If you want to put in a tiny portrait or photograph, cut it out now and glue it to the card

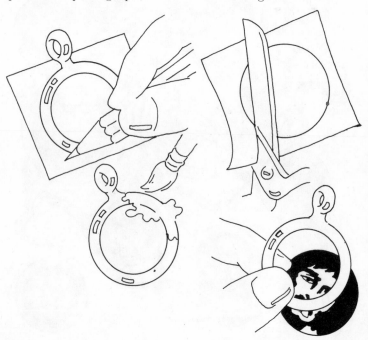

circle. Next, spread some glue on the rod ring, and place it, glued side down, on your miniature, taking care that the portrait is centred in the pendant and that the little loop ring is at the top of the picture. Leave it to dry completely and then, with a sharp pair of scissors, cut off any card that is showing round the outer edge of the ring. Thread your ribbon through the top loop and there is your pendant ready to wear.

That is the simplest way of making a pendant but there are many variations. You can paint the ring first, before glueing in your picture. Or try covering your thin card with some pretty sticky-backed flock paper or some felt. Glue your ring to this and then fill up the inside by glueing on tiny little beads collected from broken necklaces. Buy some sequins (from the dressmaking counter of most big stores) and use these to make patterns on the felt (put the glue on the sequins with a cocktail stick).

You can make a necklace by looping on several rings by knotting them into position so they do not slip; or make a medallion or fob brooch by tying a velvet bow through the little ring at the top. Sew a safety pin to the back of the bow and pin this on to a dress or a coat.

Plate People**

53

You need: 4 paper plates (2 small and 2 big if possible)
      5 red paper napkins
      4 bits of thin card, 6 cm × 6 cm (2½ ins × 2½ ins)
      4 pipe cleaners
      1 long garden cane
      rubber solution glue

These simply made paper plate people can be used as decorations at parties, to greet guests at the front door; they can be given to a child who is in bed; or simply used as giant puppets.

Here are instructions for making a Father Christmas, but you can alter the colours, the style of hat, the decorations, etc., to make other figures (a clown; a witch; a nurse; a pirate).

The cane needs to be at least 61 cm (2 ft) long. For a standing up decoration I use one 76–91 cm (2½–3 ft) in length.

To fit the face on, lay the cane on a table (or floor) between the two small paper plates, the top of the cane coming just 1 cm (½ in.) or so above the edge of the plates. Make two holes in each plate, top and bottom, on either side of the cane. Thread a pipe cleaner (or piece of wire or string) through the two holes on one side of the cane, at the top, twist it around the cane once or twice, and then thread back into the other two holes and twist the ends together. Secure the bottom of the plate in the same way.

Then lay the two bigger plates (the body) with the cane between, right next to the small ones and fix them in exactly the same way, connecting the two lots of pipe cleaners together at the neck, so that the head and body are joined.

The arms and legs are made from four red paper table napkins, which are folded in half, lengthways, in half again, and then glued together all down the length.

Put a generous amount of glue on either side of the napkin at the top, and slot the napkin in between the two larger paper plates on either side of the cane for the legs and about

5 or 6 cm (2–2½ ins) from the 'neck' for the arms. Put a little weight on the four points to help the glue to set.

Cut out simple hands and boot shapes from the thin card, making the ankles and wrists 3 cm (1¼ ins) long and slightly narrower than the width of the trousers and the sleeves. Glue the 3 cm (1¼ ins.) on both sides before sandwiching the hands and feet between the paper arms and legs.

For Father Christmas's hat, fold a red paper napkin diagonally, and glue the folded edge, before pressing it across the head, about 6 cm (2½ ins.) from the top, and joining the two ends together at the back. Glue the top corner and fold into the back.

Paint the face plate and the hands a very pale pink, and the body plates bright red. I use sticky paper, black half-circles for the eyes, red for mouth, but you could paint these in or do them in felt pen. The boots and belt are in black.

Use cotton wool for the bobble at the top of the hat, for the hair, eyebrows, moustache, beard, buttons and at the end of his sleeves and trousers. A little buckle cut from foil paper will add the finishing touches to the belt and the shoes.

If you can't get coloured table napkins use crepe paper, folded over exactly the same way as the napkins.

Christmas Flowers**

You need: *(per flower)*
    1 ping-pong ball
    1 pipe cleaner
    61 cm (2 ft) of wire (not too thin)
    tinsel
    red/green/blue cellophane paper
    paint
    glitter

An extra present which also makes a lovely centrepiece for the Christmas table.

Start with the centre of the flower. With a skewer, knitting needle or other sharp pointed object, make two holes in a ping-pong ball near the base and about 4 cm (1½ ins) apart. Thread a pipe cleaner through the holes and twist together underneath to form a 'stem'. You can now decorate the ball in several ways: paint it first and leave it like this; or, when the paint is dry, cover it with dabs of glue and shake glitter over it; or cover the ball with glue and twist tinsel around it.

Cut 61 cm (2 ft) of wire, strong enough to be a stalk, and bend one end over to form a tiny circle. You can fix the pipe cleaner stem into this very securely, by twisting it in and around the hook.

Now for the flowers. Draw around either a large plate, various sizes of round tins or trays, on the different coloured cellophane papers. Cut these out and trim the edges. Push the end of the wire stalk through the centre of a flower, dab a little glue around the middle of the flower, and pinch it together underneath the ping-pong ball. To finish off the flowers, twist some tinsel down the stalks, which you can then bend into interesting shapes. An empty milk bottle, covered in foil, makes a good vase for them.

Stick Sewing Pictures*

You need: ceiling tiles of expanded polystyrene
cocktail stick
any bits of wool
raffia
tissue paper
very lightweight material or wood

This is a fascinating way to make what looks like a sewing collage, but in fact nothing is sewn; it is all done with a cocktail stick. As it is not at all messy, it is a very good present to give to someone ill in bed, because then the patient might like to copy the idea and make some more.

I suggest that you use your first tile to experiment on, to try out various ways of making 'stitches'. First of all, break off one end of the cocktail stick, so that you have one sharp end, for working on fine wool, and one blunt end for slightly thicker wool or raffia.

To make lines of 'sewing' to look like backstitch, cut a length of wool, poke one end gently into the tile with the cocktail stick, then every centimetre or so, poke a bit of wool into the tile. If you pull too hard on any part of the wool, the whole thing comes undone extremely easily, so try to be patient and go slowly. Also, do not pierce the polystyrene too hard, or you will go through the tile.

Now for another idea, useful for grass, for making furry animals, for plants and for clothes. Cut a bit of wool, 1–2½ cms (½–1 in.), lay it flat on the tile and poke it through the middle with your cocktail stick; then the wool will stick up like a couple of blades of grass.

If you want to use thick wool, lay it out on the tile in the shape you want and lace over it in fine wool, poking from one side to the other and back again, until you have secured it firmly.

Tissue paper can be attached in this way too, and so can

very lightweight pieces of material, and even balsa wood and wooden spills or matchsticks, which you could paint first, if you cannot buy the coloured ones.

Remember that you do not have to keep the square shape of the polystyrene tile. Make an oval or a round picture within the square, perhaps painting the remaining part of the tile like a picture frame.

On the next page you will see how the finished picture looks in colour.

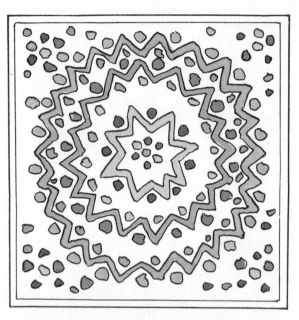

Hedgehogs★★★

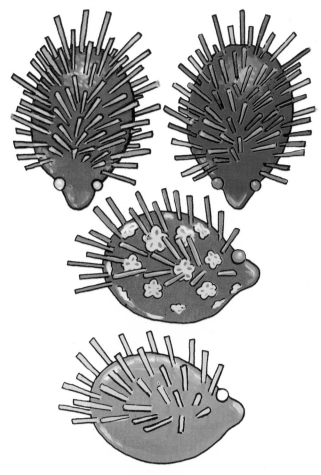

You need: 1 empty plastic lemon
about 30 cocktail sticks
2 coloured glass-headed pins
enamel paint
5 teaspoons of plaster of Paris

Once these hedgehogs are made, you forget they started life as squeezy lemons!

First, prepare the lemon by getting rid of the 'bump' made by the lid. See p. 13. Unscrew the lid, and pull out the inner tightly-fitting cap – the piece with the little hole through which the lemon is squeezed. (Use a sharp pointed knife to ease it out.) Keep the cap carefully. Now, cut off the projection immediately below the last ridge. The inner cap can now be pushed back into the hole, but before doing this, the lemon must be weighted down with plaster of Paris.

Mix 5 teaspoons of plaster with 5 teaspoons of water in a small jug, and pour it into the lemon. Push the cap on firmly and put the lemon down to let the plaster set, making sure that the lettering on the lemon is face down. If any plaster mixture dribbles out of the cap hole, squeeze some out until the level of the mixture comes to just below the hole. You can see how full it is by holding the lemon against the light. Once the plaster is completely set, shave off most of the lettering on the base, with a sharp knife or a hot blade, so that the hedgehog will stand firmly.

Paint your hedgehog all over with enamel paint. Push the two coloured glass pins in fairly close together at the front of the hedgehog (opposite end to the cap) to make his eyes.

Next, break about thirty cocktail sticks in two, to cover the top half of the animal, pushing the pointed ends into the plastic. Some of the plastic is tougher than the rest, particularly near the front and back ends, so use a hot darning needle (and wear gloves) to prepare the holes first.

For extra decoration, the prickles can be painted, or you can glue on stars or tiny flowers cut out from doilies.

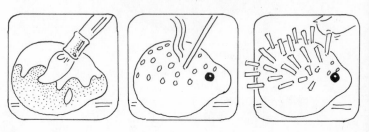

'Sweet Peas' in a Hanging Basket*

You need: empty washing-up liquid bottle
1 packet of coloured 'coasters'
green garden wire or pipe cleaners
empty cotton reel
glue and enamel or p.v.a. paint

First make the basket from an empty plastic washing-up liquid bottle. Cut the bottle along the dotted lines as illustrated (Fig. 1) with a pair of good kitchen scissors. Make two holes near the top of the container (Fig. 2) and thread a pipe cleaner or piece of wire through them. Paint it both inside and out.

Whilst you are waiting for the paint to dry, make the 'flowers'. These are made from coloured coasters which you can buy in packets. (They are used under glasses and cups to protect polished tables.) Very carefully remove the waxed backing from each coaster – you are now left with a coloured circle lined in white. Make a very small hole in the centre of

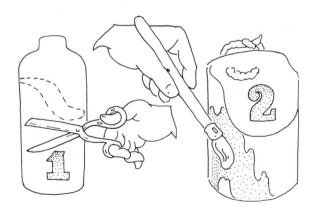

one coaster and push a pipe cleaner or piece of wire through about 1 cm ($\frac{1}{2}$ in.) (Fig. 3). Dab a little glue around the centre hole and pinch tightly underneath to form the flower (Fig. 4).

Make all your flowers in this way, keeping the white sides of the coasters as the insides of the flowers. If you buy three or four packets of different coloured coasters, you can make several baskets of mixed coloured 'Sweet Peas'.

Glue the base of an empty cotton reel and press it firmly into the bottom of the basket – or screw up a little chicken wire to fit inside, and arrange the flowers.

Sweet peas never grow with straight stems like many flowers, they twist around themselves like bindweed, so bend the wire stems into weird shapes around a pencil before arranging them in the basket.

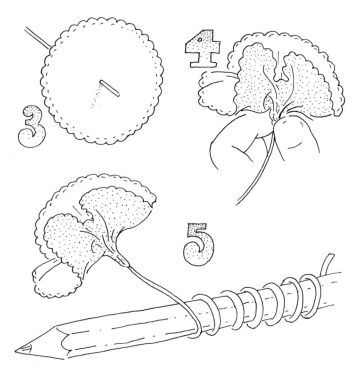

A Reminder*

You need: piece of thick cardboard, 13 cm × 20 cm
  (5 ins × 8 ins)
  2 pipe cleaners
  1 clothes peg
  decorative paper
  glue
  pencil
  61 cm (2 ft) of string

This is a sensible, practical board to hang almost anywhere in the house to write down jobs to be done: shopping lists; people to write to; telephone messages.

Cut out a piece of very thick cardboard about 13 cm × 20 cm (5 ins × 8 ins). If you have not got any really thick board, then cut out two or even three pieces of strong card, and glue them together.

Then cover the board in decorative wrapping paper or paint it or cut out pictures to cover it. If you are using wrapping paper, cut it slightly larger than the board itself (add 4 cm [1½ ins] to each side), stick the paper down on the front, turn the board over and glue the remainder on the back, taking care to fold the corners in neatly.

Make five holes in the board, with a sharp skewer, at A, B, C, D and E.

To make the hanger, thread the pipe cleaner through the front at A and B, and twist the two ends together at the back to secure.

To hold the pad of paper, push a pipe cleaner up from the back of hole C, through the wire coil of the clothes peg, and down from the front into the back of hole D. Twist the pipe cleaner together tightly at the back and cut off the spare ends. Thread the piece of string or tape through hole E, tie it in a strong knot at the back, and tie the other end to a pencil. (If you are giving this present to a right-handed relation or friend, then reverse the positions of that pencil.) Cut out some scrap paper for the note pad and clip it into the clothes peg. On the first sheet you could write: *To Alyson, to remind you what to buy, whom to write to, telephone calls to make,* or something else appropriate.

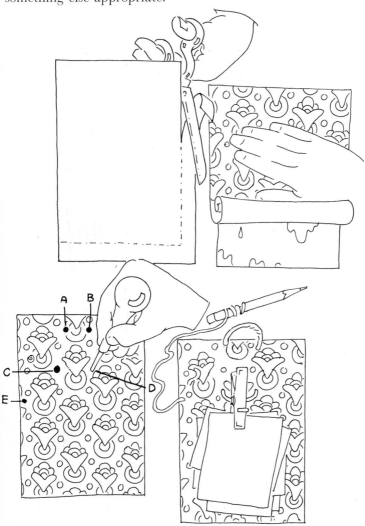

Sparkling Roses***

You need: white crepe paper
glue
cocktail sticks
white rubber bands or fuse wire or fine wire
1 ping-pong ball
1 thin stake, 30·5–36 cm (12–14 ins) long
cream or yoghurt carton
silver glitter
a few small twigs of an evergreen bush (like a bay)
if you can find some, but they are not necessary

These roses make a lovely sparkling ornament to give when flowers are expensive.

Cover a yoghurt or cream carton in silver or other coloured foil, then fill it up with damp sand or earth. Carefully make a hole in the ping-pong ball with a sharp skewer and push the stake in up to the top of the ball. Push the other end of the stake into the carton.

Now cut 8 cm (3 ins) off one end of the roll of white crepe paper. Cut up both sides where the folds are to separate each piece. Fold these in half, and again cut up the side edge to separate. To make a rounded petal shape, at one end just cut off the corners, on either side from about half way, sloping gently towards the top. Separate each petal – you will need nine petals for each flower, and about nine flowers make a little rose tree.

Because you have cut your paper widthways, it will stretch under gentle pressure; so pull all round the top half of each petal very carefully (it tears very easily) between your fingers and thumbs, and you will find that you have a nice curved shape.

With the curved side of the petal facing you, dab some glue along the bottom part. Cover just over half of a cocktail stick with glue, put the glued part down on one side of the

68

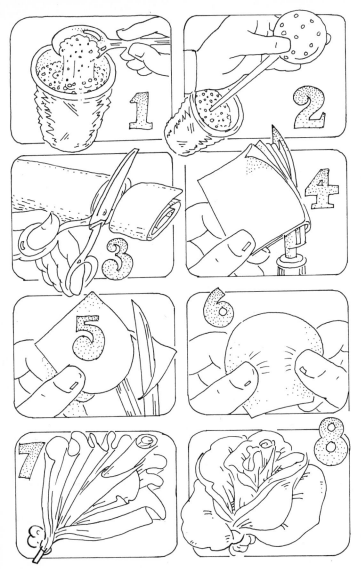

petal and roll the paper gently round the stick. Now put some glue on the base of the second petal (always on the side that curves inwards) and pinch just the base into the stick, taking care not to press the rest of the petal. Continue

putting on the other petals in this way, trying not to place one immediately behind another.

When you have finished, twist a little fuse wire or a white rubber band around the base to secure the petals firmly. Holding the flower by the band and the stick, and leaving perhaps the centre two petals, curl the remaining petals outwards, doing it fairly gradually so that the last two or three curl over quite considerably. Then dab a little glue on the edge of each petal and sprinkle on some glitter.

To cover the ping-pong ball, you will probably need to make about seven to nine flowers. If you have any gaps you want to fill, pick a few twigs of an evergreen with small leaves, make the holes in your ball with a hot skewer and push the twigs in. Finish off the present by twisting some tinsel around the stake.

If you do not want to make silver glitter roses, which are rather Christmassy, use other colours of crepe paper, or try mixing them up – deep purple with a few violet ones, or mostly red with a few pink, and leave out the glitter altogether.

Paperweights *

You need: metal jelly mould or plastic mould for sandpit toy
  cooking oil
  plaster of Paris
  poster paint
  felt
  rubber solution glue

If you have some small metal jelly moulds (perhaps in the shape of a tortoise or a rabbit) or some plastic moulds used as sandpit toys, why not use them to make paperweights?

Rub the inside of the mould with a very thin film of grease (cooking oil). Mix up some plaster of Paris, using half the quantity of water to plaster. To fill a small mould, you would probably need about 170 gms (6 oz) of plaster to 6 tablespoons (3 oz) of water. Pour this mixture into the mould and shake it gently to get a completely flat surface. Leave it to set hard. (Be sure to wash up the container you mixed the plaster in immediately you have finished using it.)

Turn the mould upside down and knock it hard once or twice. The plaster mould should come out in one piece. Leave it to dry on a wire rack.

Then paint the plaster with poster paints, and add some felt eyes and ears or any other decoration the animal needs.

Then cover the base with a thin layer of glue and press it on some felt to make a nice soft base. When the glue is set, cut away the surplus felt from around the edge.

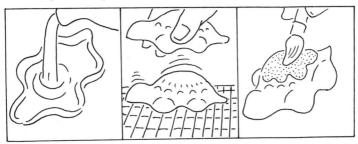

Place Markers *

You need: wafer biscuits
　　　　　rice paper
　　　　　icing sugar
　　　　　cake colouring
　　　　　cocktail sticks
　　　　　corks, or empty cotton reels

For marking guests' places at parties, try one of these ideas.
1. With a pair of small sharp pointed scissors, cut out your friend's initials from a packet of wafer biscuits and cover each wafer initial in icing sugar mixed into a coloured paste with a little cake colouring and water and spread on with a knife.
2. Ask your doctor for a large discarded syringe, fill this with coloured icing sugar (mixed to a creamy consistency so you can push it through the nozzle) and pipe your guest's names on circles cut from rice paper or on wafer biscuits.
3. Make an edible leaf print for each place setting. Wash a small well-shaped leaf, dry it thoroughly, then paint it with cake colouring. Lay it on a pad of newspaper, colour side uppermost, and press the rice paper gently on the leaf to make a printing. (Do not put too much of the colouring on the leaf because it will dissolve the rice paper.) Make several printings of different shaped leaves, but leave one corner clear to 'glue' your guest's initials, cut from a wafer.
4. Make some edible flowers to put beside each setting. Cut the rice paper into leaf or petal shapes. Decorate them with cake colouring (using as little colouring as possible and a thin paintbrush). Very gently push your leaves on to a cocktail stick, and for the centre, add a small coloured jelly tot or any other small sweet that will not break up when pierced. Individual 'flowers' can be fixed into a cork or empty cotton reel, marked with the guest's name.

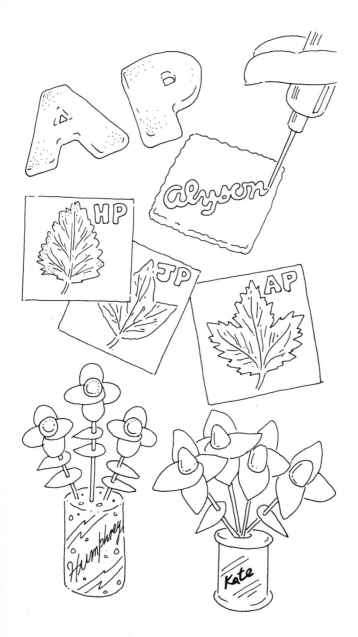

Table Decorations[*]

You need: large empty cream or yoghurt carton
stake, about 40·5 cm (16 ins) long
ping-pong ball
cocktail sticks
aluminium kitchen foil
Maltesers
marshmallows

Make two or three of these 'Malteser Trees' to put down the centre of your party table.

Cover a large cream or yoghurt carton in foil and fill it with sand or earth. Push the stake in firmly. Make a hole in the ping-pong ball with a heated skewer (insulate the end or wear gloves), and push the ball on to the stake. Press some silver foil around the ball and down the stake too if you wish, or bind the stake with ribbon or tinsel.

Very gently put one end of a cocktail stick into a Malteser and, having made a hole through the foil into the ping-pong ball with a darning needle, push the other end of the stick into this hole. Now, cover as much of the ball as you want in this way. Try mixing up marshmallows or other soft sweets with the Maltesers.

You could make a 'Cheese Tree' in the same way, cutting up small lumps of different kinds of cheese to put on the end of the sticks, or make a 'Fruit Tree' from well-drained pineapple pieces or cherries.

Another idea for a tree decoration for the party table is to make a 'Jelly Tree' for each guest. Prepare cream or yoghurt pots as with 'Malteser Trees', but put small real twigs in, and press soft jelly sweets on all possible convenient places. You must choose your twigs really well, so that you keep the pot well balanced when all the sweets are fixed on.

Fluffy Mobile***

You need: (*for each bird*)
      empty plastic lemon
      enamel paint
      feathers
      glue
      stiff card
      thread
      wire

Three or five of these fluffy birds make a pretty hanging mobile.

First, prepare the lemon by getting rid of the 'bump' made by the lid (see p. 13). Unscrew the lid, and pull out the tightly fitting inner cap – the piece with the little hole through which the lemon is squeezed (use a sharp-pointed knife to ease it out). Keep this cap carefully. Now cut off the projection immediately below the last ridge. The inner cap can now be pushed back into the hole.

With a pair of very sharp-pointed scissors, cut out a wing shape from either side of the lemon, taking great care not to cut the wing off completely (see Fig. p. 11). Cut each wing into three or four feathers. Make a hole in the centre of the plastic lettering on the lemon with a warm needle or skewer, through which to hang a thread, and with a very sharp or warm knife, cut a 2-cm ($\frac{3}{4}$ in.) slit in the top front of the lemon in which to fix the head.

Paint the lemon inside and out with enamel or p.v.a. paint.

When the paint is completely dry, tie a bit of matchwood on the end of about 20 cm (8 ins) of strong thread and dab a little glue on the knot. Now pull the thread taut through the hole you made in the plastic lettering until the matchstick is resting inside the lemon.

You can collect feathers to cover the birds from parks

where there are ducks in the pond, from butchers who pluck their own fowl, from feather dusters, or you can buy packets of feathers from some art/craft shops. Put some glue on the base of each feather and, starting at the back end of the bird, press only the base of each feather on the body, making sure each feather overlaps. Cover the top and both sides of the bird in this way, using the smallest feathers for the wings.

Draw your design for the head on the card, making the neck extra long to slot into the body and the same width as the slit you made. Paint the head and cut it out.

Tie the loose end of the thread from the bird on one end of a piece of strong wire (part of a coat hanger would do), and balance it with the two other birds. Hang up your mobile in a good draughty position.

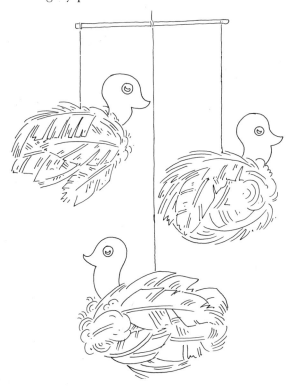

Ditty Bag***

You need: 2 tea towels
needle and strong thread
about 4·2 metres (14 ft) of tape

This is a bag of useful pockets. It is tied to the front seat of the car, but all the pockets are facing you in the back. You can fill them up with all the bits and pieces you need on a long car journey.

1. With the right side facing you, fold your first cloth in half, bringing up C + D to A + B.

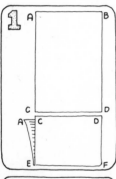

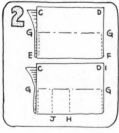

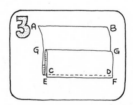

2. Mark a point exactly halfway between C to E and D to F and chalk a line across (G).

Sew the edges together between G and E, and G and F.

Mark exactly halfway across the line GG and sew down GH. Mark exactly a quarter way across and sew down GJ.

3. Now pick up the cloth at C + D and fold back to E + F. Sew all along from CE to DF (through three thicknesses). So far you have made three pockets and a pouch.

4. Take your second cloth, and with the right side facing you, fold over exactly one third of the material.

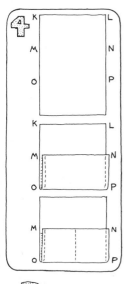

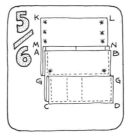

Stitch from M to O and from N to P. Mark a point halfway between M and N and sew a straight line down to the bottom.

5. Lay your second cloth out, right side facing you, and place your first cloth on top (also right side facing) matching up A to M and B to N. Sew from A to G, B to G and then right across from G to G, just *above* the flap (three thicknesses). Make quite sure not to sew the flap down at any point otherwise you will sew down the top of the pocket. You now have five pockets, a pouch and a big flap pocket.

6. Sew pieces of strong tape (about 70 cm [28 in.] long) to the places marked with a * (eight altogether).

7. Tie your ditty bag to the front seat of the car.

Here are some suggestions for filling it: pad of paper; pencils; comics; book of car games; playing cards; sweets; toy matchbox cars; teddy; little dolls; damp flannel or washcloth in a small polythene bag; paper handkerchiefs; water bottle, paperback books; maps; flashlight; pocket chess.

*Topical Tree**

You need: 5 cardboard tubes (from lavatory paper rolls or
        paper towels)

        strong card, 22 cm (8 ins) square

        paint

        strong glue

        a stapler if possible

        little pictures or photographs

Make this tree to frame lots of topical pictures. Use photographs of the family, pop stars, footballers, characters cut
from comics.

Cut fifteen circles, each 2·5 cm (1 in.) wide, from paper
towel or lavatory paper rolls. From your piece of strong card
cut a strip 2·5 cm (1 in.) wide by 18 cm (7 ins) long. Find
the exact centre of this card and to it staple, or glue, a circle;
then staple or glue two more circles on either side of this
central one, and staple or glue them to each other at the
sides as well.

On top of this line, staple four more circles to fit into the
four hollows of the first line, and staple them to each other as
well. Follow this with a line of three circles, then two, then a
single circle on top.

Now glue the entire shape to a strong upright, making a
trunk. You can make the tree as small or as tall as you wish, but
15 cm (6 ins) upright (paper towel roll) gives a good height.

When the top of the tree is firmly fixed to the trunk, paint
the entire tree inside and out. Let the paint dry completely,
then lay the circles down on your card and, with a pencil,
mark around the inside of each circle on the card, taking
care not to move the tree whilst you are drawing. Now you
will see where to glue each picture on the card.

When you have chosen the order in which you want to
place your pictures, start at the top and draw the shape of
the inside of the top circle on the picture you have chosen
to fill it. Cut the circle around the picture 2 mm ($\frac{1}{8}$ in.)

bigger than you have drawn it, and glue it on the card in the correct marked position. Fill up the other fourteen circles in this way.

Now cover the back of the tree in glue. This means the back of each circle and the back of the strip of card (not the trunk), and press the glued part carefully on your prepared card, arranging the 'frames' carefully to fit centrally over the pictures. With the tree still lying flat, place a weight on it (an iron) until the glue is firmly set.

Then cut the card away all around the outside of the tree.

You can make a very pretty tree with arrangements of tiny dried flowers set into each frame – or with a collection of coins or badges.

Button Pictures^{*}

You need: lots of different sized buttons
glue
the lid of a chocolate or cheese box
felt or hessian
paint
gold or silver braid of any sort

You can make beautiful pictures and designs with buttons glued to a dark background and set in a frame.

Collect together all the odd buttons you can find. If you cannot find enough, you can buy little buttons in a variety of colours at most good haberdashery counters.

Button pictures show up best against a dark plain cloth background, like felt, adhesive felt or a material such as hessian or burlap. The lid of a chocolate box or a circular or

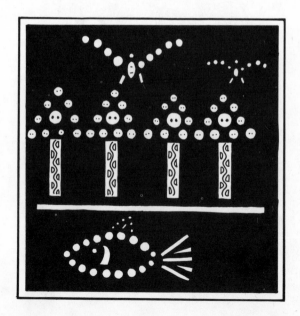

square cheese box will make good frames within which to work.

Paint the outside of the box lid, giving it two or three coats to cover any writing or design. You can also paint the inside rim of the box if you do not want to cover it with material. When the paint is dry, glue on your material to the inside base of the box. Now, spend some time trying out your ideas on the material. Because the circular shape of buttons limits your design, put some flow and movement into the picture by adding different varieties of gold or silver braid or trimmings. (You can buy a very small amount of braid at the dressmaking counter of any good store, and you can use the braid alone or pull out the different strands that have been plaited together.) To fix these, put the glue on the background material with a cocktail stick and press the trimmings on carefully.

Use the braid for such things as stems and leaves of flowers, plants and trees, to give the impression of water, or as a walking stick, the handle of an umbrella, string for balloons, handlebars on a bicycle or pram, the spikey parts of a prehistoric monster, or the ropes on a swing or a hammock.

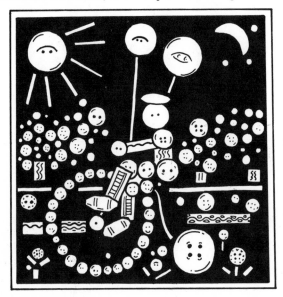

Sparkling Trees ★ ★

You need: polystyrene ceiling tile   glitter
small size paper fasteners   glue

Start with a simple triangle-shape tree. Draw this on a
polystyrene tile and cut it out, either with the proper tool (a
battery-run cutter) or with the point of a sharp knife, and
gently break away the unused pieces. Carefully push paper
fasteners all round the inside edge of the tile, leaving as big
or as small a gap as you want. Cover the top of each paper
fastener with glue, taking *great* care that none spills on
to the tile, and shake the glitter over the paper fasteners.

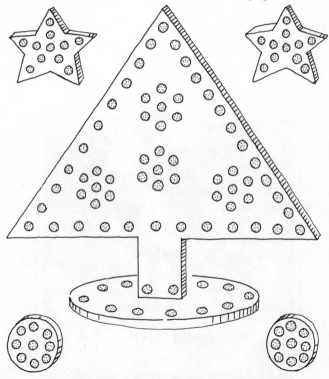

After a minute or two, blow the rest of the glitter off very carefully on to some paper (so that you can use it again).

When you have seen the super glittering effect this has, try some other tree or even star shapes, and put different sparkling designs on them.

If you want to use different coloured glitters to make patterns on the same tree, do each lot of colours separately, letting one colour dry completely before starting on another otherwise your glitters will get mixed.

To make a base, so that the trees can stand upright, cut a piece from the remains of the tile and make a hole in the centre of it just big enough to wedge the trunk in tightly.

You can decorate the stars on the back and the front if you want to hang them on your Christmas tree, provided that the paper fasteners are small enough not to go through the other side. Hang them up by a thread.

*Pasta Pictures**

You need: a piece of strong card
              paint
              hessian or felt
              glue
              pasta, lentils etc.
              silver or gold aerosol spray

For the base of your picture, paint a piece of stiff cardboard or cover it with felt or hessian. A dark colour gives the best results.

Then collect together all sorts of differently shaped pastas – macaroni, spaghetti, shells, wagon wheels, as well as lentils, rice, haricot beans, and split peas. Make up your design carefully, trying out all sorts of ideas. Then, when it is ready, glue on each piece using a cocktail stick to help with the tricky parts.

When the glue is firmly set, you can spray your picture with silver or gold aerosol. But, with a little more trouble, you can make the picture even more effective by spraying only the pasta and beans etc. To do this cover the background with bits of newspaper, torn roughly to fit into all the odd shapes and corners, but do not worry if parts of the background get painted. The force of the aerosol spray can lift the pieces of newspaper, so stick pins in at strategic points to help keep the paper firmly in place. When the spraying is finished, take the pins out and carefully lift off the scraps of paper.

To finish, fix a tag on the back with strong sellotape or glue, so that the picture can be hung up.

Sparkling Shapes ★★

You need: a packet of gummed reinforcements or cloth rings
glue
glitter
thread

An unbelievably simple way to make gorgeous decorations for the Christmas tree, to hang in a window or across a room, to brighten up parcels, to paste on to Christmas cards (and to make beautiful fake jewellery, particularly for plays). The reinforcements you need are sold in packets or small boxes from most newsagents – they are used for strengthening the holes in loose-leaf paper. Do work on a large plate or tin tray, as the rings do not stick so easily to it as they would to paper.

Lay one ring down, sticky side facing you. Lick half of another ring and place it (sticky side up) under the first so that it just comes to the inner edge of the first circle. Press down with the back of a pencil or pen (less apt to stick than your hands).

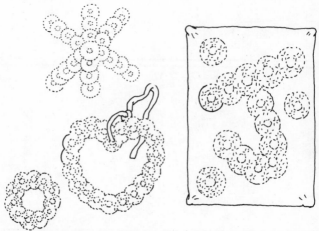

Continue in this way until you have formed the design you want (star, circle, tree, bell, etc.). Leave the shape to dry, then, when it feels quite firm, paint glue gently all over one side, and cover with silver glitter. When this has set, gently glue the other side and cover in glitter.

If you are making Sparkling Shapes to decorate a Christmas card or parcel, then you need put glitter only on one side.

To make a present look something special, wrap it up in plain bright-coloured paper, and glue on the recipient's initials (made in the same way as the decoration).

*Paper Plate Pockets**

You need: 1½ paper plates
60–70 cm (2 ft) of string or cord
some wool or raffia

Cut a paper plate in half, join one of these halves to a whole plate, and you can quickly make an extremely useful pocket. Add some string and hang it up in the kitchen for odd recipes; in the car as a rubbish pocket; in the garden shed to hold seed packets; in your bedroom for cotton wool, paper handkerchiefs; use it for the dog's brush and comb, or make it into a small child's bag. Fill up the pocket with appropriate things for an unusual present.

First, join the half plate to the whole plate with the right sides facing each other. This means, if you have chosen coloured plates, the colour will be on the inside.

You can fit the plates together in a variety of ways: blanket stitch them with bright wool or raffia (and continue the stitching right round the rest of the plate as well); or use narrow ribbon or tape and an overlapping stitch. If you have a stapler, you can fix the plates firmly together before adding the stitching. Add some cord so that you can hang the pockets up.

Decorate the plates with felt pen or paint; or glue on pictures cut from magazines, seed catalogues or wrapping paper.

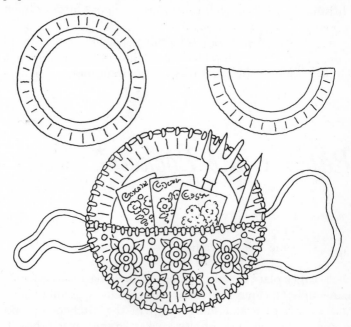

Foil Flowers★★

You need: a ping-pong ball
a strong thin stake, about 40 cm (16 ins) long
a pipe cleaner and some thin wire (fuse wire)
a strip of coloured foil paper 12 cm (4¾ ins) by 20 cm (8 ins) and some scraps for leaves
a long piece of kitchen foil, 52 cm (20½ ins) by 30 cm (11¾ ins), and one piece 12 cm (4¾ ins) square
narrow strips of green crepe paper, 9 cm (4¾ ins)
cream or yoghurt pot
glue

These are large, bright sparkling flowers made from silver kitchen foil, each one standing in its own pot.

Start with the centre of the flower. Make three holes in a ping-pong ball, all in a straight line, 1 cm (½ ins) between each hole. (Do this with a sharp-pointed pair of scissors or a heated skewer.) Thread a pipe cleaner or a piece of wire through the two outer holes and push the stick right up the centre one.

Cut out a 12 cm (4¾ ins) square from your kitchen foil, and cover the ping-pong ball with it, securing the foil at the base first with glue and also by twisting the pipe cleaner or wire around both it and the stick.

Next, cut a strip of coloured foil paper 12 cm (4¾ ins) by 20 cm (8 ins). Fold this in half (6 cm (2½ ins) by 20 cm (8 ins)) and make it into a frill by cutting narrow strips, 4 cm (1½ ins) in length, starting at the top folded edge. Put some glue all along the uncut part of the foil, and gently press this around the stick at the base of the ping-pong ball.

Now cut a piece of silver kitchen foil, 52 cm (20½ ins) by 30 cm (11¾ ins), fold this in half (52 cm (20½ ins) by 15 cm (6 ins)) making sure that the shiny side of the foil is on the outside. Starting at the folded edge, cut slits 2½ cm (1 in.) wide and 10 cm (4 ins) long to make the petals. Trim each petal at the top to give the petals a good shape.

Spread glue all over the uncut part of the foil and press this part of the flower around the base of the coloured foil on the stick, easing the foil gently, so that the petals in the second row show between those in the first row. As each petal is made from two layers of foil you can easily shape it with your fingers to curl outwards, or upwards, but leave this part of the arranging until the end, as the petals break off fairly easily. Press the whole of the base tightly together.

To make the leaves, cut out three or four leaf shapes from coloured foil paper, each shape cut double, and glue the insides of each leaf together with a piece of thin wire running up the centre and 10 cm (4 ins) or so left hanging at the base. Twist the remaining wire around the stake where you want your leaf to sprout.

Finally, cut several strips of green crepe paper, 1 cm ($\frac{1}{2}$ in.) by 30 cm (11$\frac{3}{4}$ ins). Make sure to cut the paper 'on the stretch'. Put dabs of glue all the way down a strip, and twist it around the stake, starting at the top and covering the base of the foil flower.

Plant your foil flower in a 9 cm (3$\frac{1}{2}$ ins) flower pot filled with earth or sand – or in a cream carton that you have disguised with pretty paper. Then gently arrange your foil petals.

Some other non-fiction Puffins

The Big Book of Puzzles   *Michael Holt and Ronald Ridout*
The Boomerang Book   *M. J. Hanson*
Cooking is a Game You Can Eat   *Fay Maschler*
Fun with Collage   *Jan Beaney*
Fun with Paper Modelling   *G. C. Payne*
How to Survive   *Brian Hildreth*
The Insects in your Garden   *Harold Oldroyd*
The Junior Puffin Quiz Book   *Norman and Margaret Dixon*
The Paper Aeroplane Book   *Seymour Simon*
Paper Folding and Modelling   *Aart van Breda*
Paper World   *Clive Manning*
Puffin Book of Freshwater Fishing   *Roger Pierce*
The Puffin Book of Magic   *Norman Hunter*
The Puffin Crossword Puzzle Book   *Alan Cash*
The Puffin Quiz Book   *Norman and Margaret Dixon*
The Puffin Soccer Quiz Book   *David Prole*
The Puffin Song Book   *compiled by Leslie Woodgate*
Something to Do   *Septima*
Something to Make   *Felicia Law*
Things to Do   *Hazel Evans*